LAWS OF THE STREET
- The Madness Begins -
Vol. 1

Written by Lamont Carey

Edited by
Sharon Coker

Book design and graphics
Created by
J. P. Lago

Photo of Lamont Carey
taken by
Rashidah Denton

D1488646

LAWS Of The STREET. Vol. 1

Copyright © 2019 by Lamont Carey

All rights reserved. The reproduction, transmission or utilization of this work in whole or in part in any form by any electronic, mechanical or other means, now known or hereafter invented, including xerography, photocopying and recording, or in any information storage or retrieval system, is forbidden without written permission. For permission, please contact Lamont Carey at LaCarey

Entertainment, LLC-P.O.
Box 64256, Washington,
DC 20029 U.S.A.
Twitter: @lamontcarey
Facebook:
LaCareyentertainment,llc/
lamontcarey
Distributed Worldwide
ISBN-13: 978-1-945806-
05-6

Special thanks

Pharaoh, Joshua, Elijah, Philip, Khaleel, Libra Mayo, Robert & Ella, Tracy, T. Brooks, Mark H., Holli, Jenny K., Lady Flava, Sharon Coker, Brenda Richardson, Bianca "Mz. B" Brown, Lisa Lindsey, Carrie, Jermaine Ingram, Lil Tye, Bunmi Love, Jessica, Hermond Palmer, Michelle B, Vanette Rosser, Francia Baker, Wendy H., Robert Robertson, The Laws Of The STREET Cast and Crew, and to all the individuals who have supported my work by encouraging me to live my dreams. Special shout out to the men in women in correctional facilities around the world that write to me to encourage me. You started this journey for me. The dream is real.

"Keep Your Hustle but Change Your Product

Dear Reader

Thank you for giving my work an opportunity to become a part of your reading experience. My goal is that you not only enjoy this book and my others; it is my hope that it inspires you and provides you with additional understanding of the challenges that individuals and communities face on a daily. I hope you feel encouraged to get involved, change your own actions, be inspired to express yourself and live your dreams.

You have enabled me to not only live my dream of

being a business owner, author and motivational speaker but also to engage you during my lifetime. Thank you for being such a significant part of my life. You are a part of my inspiration. You are reading this book whether you purchased it or checked it out at a library, I am aware that you wanted to read my work.

I made a lot of horrible choices as a youth that lead me to prison. In prison is where I found my gift to tell stories, from my bad choices is where I learned the stories that I would later write about and now I make my living from turning bad choices into all forms of communication. What I hope that you get out of this is that it is never too late to live your dream or too change. The problem is that too many people convince us that our mistakes are unrepairable. We may not be able to undo the mistakes we have made but learning from them helps us to never repeat them. Moreover, YOU are capable of being anything you want to be. You just have to find it in yourself to LIVE your dream and the best way to do that is to GO AFTER IT! Don't talk about it, study it forever, ask a thousand questions forever! You have to live it and learn from the mistakes. The only way to be successful is to go after success with actions and not hope. I believe in you just like you believe in me. We can do and become anything. Let's become that person we envision we could be...because you can be exactly that person. It lives in you now. Release it!!!

I hope you are willing to do a few things for me. Here they are: take a picture of you reading the book, email it to me at lacareymanagement@gmail.com and post it on social media, write your thoughts on the book on amazon/my website: lacareyenterprise.com/reviews

Check out the questions at the end.

Sincerely,
Lamont Carey

CHAPTER 1

The night sky squeezes the stars until they twinkle and the moon glares down on the bridge running across 295 Interstate in Washington, DC. The light traffic zips up and down both lanes passing the Benning Road exit. Next to 295 a mixture of impatient and relaxed people waits on the subway platform for the train. On the opposite side of 295 is Lucky Seven, a 24-hour store, positioned in the foreground of the dark, low-income apartment complexes known as The Fair and The Dwellings Apartments. The apartment complexes have thousands of residents. The Fair has a black metal gates that wraps around the whole complex. The gates resemble prison bars, but without the barbwires running across the top. Across the street from The Fair are new row-houses and a middle school. There is a small church, with no surrounding lights, with a 20-car parking lot behind it. The church looks dark and creepy. The store is the only lit spot in the vicinity. The streetlights are even dim. The bridge stands firm as the only escape route from the deprived residents seeking escape.

It curves like the body of a snake and the entrance exposes them to the dangerous traffic. A medical clinic hides in the shadow of the bridge on the apartments side of the interstate.

Madness is concealed against the side of the bridge near the entrance but facing the medical clinic. His cell phone rings. He answers it as a train can be heard coming in his direction on other side of the interstate.

"Yea...O.K. I am waiting for you now. See you in a few seconds, Baby." He hangs the phone up and tucks it

in his pocket. He waits eight minutes before peeping out the shadows and looks up at the bridge. He notices one figure walking across the highway portion of the bridge. He sees another figure at least ten feet behind the first. Madness leans back into the shadow until he hears footsteps above his head. He leans out and sees the back of a male walking down the ramp. He leans back into the shadow. A minute later he peers out and sees the male getting closer to the exit of the ramp. He notices the woman walking above his head on the ramp.

The man exits the ramp and heads into the shadow towards Madness. He doesn't notice him. Madness presses his back as hard as he can against the wall. Then he starts walking along the wall, concealing himself as he slowly walks toward him. As the woman exits the ramp, the man is within three feet of Madness. They are almost pass each other before Madness slams his fist against the man's face. The man crashes into the wall. He tries to push himself up as one of his knees hits the ground. On the way up, Madness shoots him once in the side of his face. The man's body slumps to the ground. Madness stoops over top of him and fires two more shots into the man's FACE. Then he stands and holds his free hand out to the woman:

"Come, Baby; we have to get out of here." He says with urgency.

In total shock. She cannot move.

"Come on, Baby; we have to go." He says with more urgency.

She looks at him in terror, but he can't see anything but her frame. She's distraught but regains her composure.

She reaches her hand to him as she steps toward him. He fires one shot into her stomach. She whines and clenches her stomach as she stumbles backward. She looks at him with confusion as he steps forward and fires another shot into her forehead. Her head jerks backward as she slumps to the ground. He stoops and sees her dead eyes staring up at him. He puts the gun in his pocket and pulls the ski-mask off his face. He then walks across the street into the first apartment complex. He follows a walkway that leads to the back of the building. A car starts and he gets into the front passenger seat.

Light Skin is the driver. His white t-shirt and the whites of his eyes are the only things visible on his dark skin.

Madness leans his slim frame against the headrest as he runs his hand over his baldhead, cameral complexion face and barely visible goatee.

"Is the city safer?" The 28-year-old says humorously as his sparkling white teeth appear.

The 17-year-old, Madness, places the gun in Light Skin's palm. *"It is now."* He replies.

"My man." Light Skin says as he lays the gun on his lap. Madness lies back in his seat and the car drives out of the parking space.

CHAPTER 2

The morning air is soothing. The playground is in the center of The Fair's gigantic apartment complex. There is a black top off to the right side of the playground. Fall leaves lie silent on the ground. Slim is seated across the top of one of three park benches positioned around the playground. He is a slender twenty-six-year-old man with a regular haircut. He glances around him and sees no other soul in sight as he toys with his cellular phone. O.G. walks out from in between two of the buildings behind him and down the narrow concrete walkway. He is an older man in his fifties. He's slim, tall and wears cheap round black framed prescription eyeglasses. He walks toward Slim. Slim senses him and glances over his shoulder. A broad grin surfaces on Slim's face as he stands. They embrace. O.G scans the area before passing him a quarter ounce of powder cocaine wrapped in a clear plastic bag.

Slim retakes his seat and O.G. stands near him. Slim fake coughs in his hand but he is really looking at the drugs. *"O.G., what do I suppose to do with this*? I'm not going back to jail for this." He says seriously.

"You're welcome. Slim, my money is funny. Business is not as good as it was. Why didn't you call me three months ago when you first came home?" O.G. says with disappointment.

"Because I was trying to stay out of trouble." Slim replies, jokingly.

They both chuckle.

"I'm hurt." O.G. replies as he continues to laugh.

"So why you struggling?" Slim questions.

O.G.'s smile vanishes too. *"One, the white man has his foot on my neck. Then Light Skin and these youngsters are hiding the connects."*

"What youngsters?" Slim says.

"They new. However, there are a few of them running around here getting money...Anyway, I'm sure if you holla at Light Skin, he'll do you better than what I just offered."

"You know me and dat man ain't on that type of time." Slim says as he stands and puts his hands in his pockets. He spits on

the ground as he glances
around the area.

*"That was a long time ago.
He's not thinking about
that anymore."* O.G. says
reassuringly.

*"Anyway, I want to see
these youngsters."* Slim
replies.

"Why? What's up?" O.G.
says with suspicion.

*"It might be time for them
to start paying taxes."* Slim
says as he spits again.

CHAPTER 3

The noon sun sets above this old-abandoned school, blocked in by low-income housing and a graveyard. Light Skin is a few inches below the three- pointer line on the basketball court that is connected to Malcolm X Elementary school. The flamboyant nine-teen year old M.T. is in front of him trying to block the shot. Nineteen-year-old Derrick's plaits are bouncing as he tries to outsmart twenty-one-year-old Earl who is trying to keep away from the basketball. Twenty-three-year-old Donny is being checked by a

nineteen-year-old
Rob. Light Skin shoots the
ball. The ball hits the
backboard and bounces
away from the court. Light
Skin bends over
exhausted. M.T. walks up
and smacks him on the
butt.

*"All of a sudden you got
asthma! Don't die yet,
Light Skin. One more point
and it is game!!!!"* M.T
laughs.

Derrick walks over
to Light Skin. Donny is
picking up the ball off the
ground.

Earl is laughing as
he points at Light Skin. He

moves when Derrick moves. *"Why are you selling your team out?"*

Light Skin continues to try to catch his breath. *"Ya will never score! I'm checking you now!"* Light Skin says.

Earl raises his arms in victory. *"GAME!!!"* He shouts.

Light Skin stands up. *"Whatever!!! Play ball...Derrick, switch! I'm checking Earl."*

Rob shouts as he walks outside the line around the court, *"I'm taking it out!"*

Madness is standing on the sideline beside Precious. She is a gorgeous twenty-five-year-old woman with a light complexion and long wavy hair. She is seated in a folding chair. She looks bored but relaxed.

Slim stroll onto the court ahead of O.G. He looks back at O.G. *"Isn't that Little Corey?"*

"He's not Little Corey anymore. He's Madness." O.G. replies as Slim stops and faces him.

"What? Madness!!?" Slim says laughing with an amused look.

Without smiling, O.G. stares into his eyes, *"Yeah, he's doing hits for Light Skin now."*

"What? Nawwwww." Slim says in glee. He walks briskly over to Madness and rubs the back of the young man's head, playfully. Madness spins as he reaches under his shirt for his gun. He grabs the handle and stares threateningly at Slim.

"Go head. Try your hand." Slim's smile quickly fades into anger as he stares daringly into his eyes.

Precious leaps up and sprints away from them.

"Don't you ever put your motherfucking hands on me again!!" Madness barks as he glares into his eyes.

"What? Do you know who you talking to?" Slim says with more anger.

"Yea. I know who the fuck you are, but you heard what the fuck I said!" Madness shouts back as he leans his face closer to Slim and tightens his grip on his gun but not pulling it out.

Light Skin runs over and jumps in between them. He separates them with his palms.

"You don't want it." Slim threatens as he tries to move around Light Skin toward Madness.

Madness's arm motions as he tries to pull the gun out of the waist of his pants. M.T. grabs Madness's wrist hand that is on the gun. Donny tugs at Madness shoulder on the other side. O.G. whispers in Slim's ear as he gently tugs at him to walk away. *"Let that go."* O.G. says.

"Chill out, ya!" Light Skin barks at Madness.

"He better learn quick that shit has changed around here." Madness shouts as

O.G. continues to ease Slim away. Slim immediately tries to dart toward Madness. O.G. grabs him around his shoulders

"Little Corey, you better stop smelling yoself!" Slim says with a sinister tone.

Light Skin presses one hand against Madness chest as he extends his other arm out in the direction of Slim. Rob and M.T. are still holding onto Madness.
"Keep talking! Keep talking and you will take your last motherfucking smell!" Madness says in rage.

Slim pulls away from O.G. but O.G. immediately grabs hold of him around his waist.

"You threatening me!? You threatening me!?" Slim screams.

"Now what?" Madness says in a calmer but threatening tone.

"Madness! Go for a walk! Now!" Light Skin commands.

Madness jerks his arms free of the men holding him. *"Get the fuck off of me."* The men step back as he walks to the far end of the court.

Light Skin takes a deep breath then walks over to Slim. *"I'm sorry about that, Slim. He has a little temper. I'll talk to him and squash that."* Light Skin says with sympathy.

Slim snatches himself free from O.G. He stares at Light Skin, *"I don't need you to squash shit for me!"* He says before walking off the court in the opposite direction of Madness.

"Talk to your man." Light Skin says with a silent warning to O.G.

O.G. nods his head in agreement before

following Slim off of the
court.

CHAPTER 4

Crud and Little Man are walking into The Fair apartment complex where they live. They see Faith and two other nine-year-old girls sitting on one of the apartment steps, gossiping. They head toward them.

Little Man is a 15-year-old very light complexion fat kid with long dreads and a beard. His dreads are wrapped around the top of his head and tied in a bow that is stationary at the center of the back of his head. Faith has a light complexion with long brownish and reddish hair that stops in-between her shoulder blades. Her hair is tied in a plaits.

Crud speeds up his pace and in a playfully threatening tone, as he steps up onto the steps in front of them, *"Where your sista at?"* The 15-year-old demands. Little Man stops at the bottom of the steps.

Faith looks at him, frowns and rolls her eyes. The other girls stare with mixed expressions of fear and curiosity. *"Excuse you. Who are you? Who are you talking too?"* Faith says with her little hands on her hips and her fearless light hazel eyes glaring at him.

"Little Girl don't play with me. I'ma grown ass man. Now where your sista at?" He leans threateningly but playfully over her, causing her to lean wayyyyyyy back before she steps onto the step above him.

Little Man walks up to him.

"Hey, Lit-tle Maaaaan." She says blushing and batting her eyes.

He's completely uncomfortable. He dismissively waves to her.

Her girlfriends start giggling which causes her to blush even more.

"Your little grown ass heard me talking to you!" Crud says snapping his finger in front of her eyes.

She rolls her eyes from Little Man to Crud. She pats her pockets. *"What!! My sista is not in my pocket!"* She looks at her little friends and shakes her head with a look that says, they are pathetic. He frowns and shakes his head with a look of hatred. Little Man smirks as they start walking off.

"And my sista does not like you!" She shouts at Crud.

Crud spins around and stares angrily at her. The little girls laugh. He scurries around looking at the ground. He picks up some pebbles and starts throwing them at the girls. Little Man tries to stop him, but he moves and continues to launch the pebbles at them. The girls run, screaming into the building.

CHAPTER 5

Slim is leaning with his back on the doorframe of the car. He is standing in between the open front passenger door and the frame of O.G.'s older model BMW. He is outside the school's basketball court where he got into a confrontation with Madness a few minutes earlier. He stares angrily over at Madness who is standing beside Precious sixty yards away inside the fenced in basketball court.

Madness and Precious are watching Light Skin, Donny, M.T.,

Rob, Derrick, and Earl as they continue to play basketball. Light Skin smacks the ball away as Earl attempts to shooting the ball into one of the baskets, but Earl recovers the ball.

O.G. is leaning on the closed back door beside Slim. *"He i-s not worth it. He's just a youngin trying to be a man"* O.G. says in a sympathizing but rationalizing tone.

"But why would he act like that on me? I can't believe Little Corey." Slim says with a simmer of anger but more disappointment.

"That's just it. He's not Little COREY anymore." O.G. reminds.

"I know...He's Madness, the killer. Did you see how they all ran and grabbed him like he's a threat? Who were those dudes anyway?" Slim says with a look of bewilderment.

"He is a threat. His body count is pretty significant from what I hear. Now two of the other guys work for Light Skin. The other three they were playing against are some of the youngins I was telling you about. They're making a little money. They actually are some good little dudes."

O.G replies with a degree
of being proud of them.

*"How they some good
dudes when you
struggling?"* Slim says
with disregard.

*"I'm doing ok. I'll be back
on my feet...especially with
you being home."* O.G. says
jokingly but with serious
undertones as he pats
Slim on his shoulder.

"I need a hammer?" Slim
says as he stares in the
direction of Madness.

"Don't do that to that kid."
O.G. says with sympathy.

The crowd on the basketball court erupts into cheers and groans as Earl makes a shot from the three- pointer range.

"GAME!!!" Earl shouts in full pride mode as he backs up and throws his arms in the air in victory, but his fingers pointing down as he walks back looking into Light Skin's disappointed eyes. Then his team leaps up and down on him in victory.

Slim and O.G watch the celebration. The losers walk off the court toward Madness and Precious in disappointment. Light Skin tugs her shoulder as he steps a few feet behind her chair. She turns into him. He speaks to her briefly before she exits the court and walks toward O.G. and Slim. The two men watch her. As she gets closer, Slim and her lock eyes, admiringly. She then walks across the street over to the driver side of a Range Rover parked in front of several luxury cars. The cars are parked in front of the low-income apartments. She leans into the backseat before exiting the truck carrying a backpack. She stares into Slim's eyes as she crosses the street. Then she walks with a switch as she re-enters the court.

"Don't repeat the past."
O.G. says with humor.

"I didn't do anything." Slim
says with a hint of
amusement.

"I saw the looks." O.G.
replies.

Slim keeps watching
her as she hands Light
Skin the backpack. He
retrieves a few large
stacks of money out of the
bag and hands them to
M.T. M.T. begins to count
the money. Light Skin
playfully shoves him. They
both start laughing. Then
Madness turns and he and
Slim lock eyes.

"I need a hammer," Slim says in almost a whisper.

CHAPTER 6

The day has settled and the sunlight that poured into Mrs. Janice's window blinds and thin yellow see-through curtains has vanished. The living room has a 1950s feel. There is a large plant on the opposite sides of the tan and striped sofa that is positioned in front of the window. All of the furniture is tan. A matching couch rest against the wall near the sofa. Across from the couch is a huge box TV screen. On opposite sides of the TV are two four level stands with family pictures. Above the TV is a picture of a white Jesus at the Last Supper. In the center of the floor is a narrow living room table with a ceramic white Swan resting on a white knitted round cloth with yellow trimming.

Mrs. Janice is seated comfortably at the table inside of her small kitchen. The kitchen is connected to the living room. She is a full-figured woman with shiny gray hair. She looks like a mean grandmother. Seated next to her is 16-year-old Little Bible Study. He is a slender and short teenager with shoulder length plaits with an upper-body and neck full of tattoos. He has three full color teardrop tattoos on the bottom corner of his left eye.

They both have their Bibles open.

"And behold, I am coming quickly, and My reward is with Me, to give to everyone according to his work. I am the Alpha and the Omega, the Beginning and The End, the First and the Last-" Little Bible Study reads before being interrupted.

Praise God! Praise God, Baby." Mrs. Janice says with a look of fulfillment. She leans forward and kisses him on the cheek and grabs his hands as she stands. He follows suit. Then she hugs him with the affection of a proud mother. *"I am so proud of you. You are becoming stronger and stronger in your walk with Christ,"* she says before hugging him again, *"Praise God."*

"I feel the strength daily. It is a struggle sometimes but when I call on the Lord for strength, I am rescued." He says with conviction.

"You keep calling on him, you hear me?" She says smiling and nudging him toward the living room.

"Yes, Ma'am. He says without budging.

"There will always be temptations. So, don't you give in. You have come a long way, and I am really proud of you. I just pray that my son finds the Lord in my lifetime." She says in earnestly as she nudges him toward the living room. He begins to walk slowly in that direction. Then he stops.

"I am sure he will. He has been keeping his distance from the Streets. He's trying. Remain patient with him." Little Bible Study responds.

"God bless your heart..."
She says as she motions
him to the door. He stops
near the doorknob.

*"Can we pray before I
leave? I can see the
concern in your eyes for
your son. I just want you to
remain at peace and be
reassured God has watch
over him. Now let's pray."*
He says.

She places her
hands in his.

CHAPTER 7

The starless night sky covers the thousands of tombstones that are spread throughout the graveyard. Light Skin's truck is barely visible as it sits on a narrow road that slopes and divides the cemetery grounds. The truck is running. He is seated behind the steering wheel, nodding his head to hardcore rap music. All of the tinted windows are rolled up except for the passenger window. It is half rolled down.

Movement catches his attention. The figure slowly comes into view. It is Madness dressed in all black. He is walking slowly in deep thought as he passes tombstones on his way toward the truck. He starts wiping his hands on his pants as he glances around before climbing into the passenger seat. Light Skin holds out his hand. *"You ok now?"* He says with concern.

Madness smirks and nods his head. *"Yea. I'm good."* Madness replies.

Light Skin nods. The passenger window rolls up as Madness leans back into his seat. Light Skin backs the truck up on the grass and drives back down the dark road.

CHAPTER 8

Hours later, Slim sneaks into the dark house. He tries to gently lock the door behind him. It makes a loud clicking sound as it locks. He hears the bedroom door open and the living room light almost instantaneously turns on. He frowns before turning around to see his mother leaning on the wall near her bedroom and living room. Her hair is in rollers and she has on a white fluffy robe.

"Hey, Ma'? I'm sorry if I woke you up." He says

without taking a step
away from the door.

She gives him a
sympathetic smirk as she
walks over and motherly
caresses his cheek. Her
eyes never leaving his. He
drops his eyes from hers.
*"I was up. How was your
day?"* Mrs. Janice says.

"It was o.k." He says
without looking up at her.

*"Don't get discouraged,
Baby. You will find a job. I
have prayed on it?"* She
says as she raises his
chin.

He looks at her with
concern. *"O.k.
Thanks."* Before he side-

steps her and walks into the kitchen and begins looking inside of the refrigerator.

"One of them jobs will call and tell you-you are hired. I left you some money on the table in here. It's enough to get you around on the bus tomorrow." She says.

He peers at her over the refrigerator door. *"Ma,"* he says with irritation.

"I don't want to hear it. You can pay me back when you get a job. As a matter of fact, you can pay all my bills." She says with a twirl of her finger as she laughs

and walks back into her bedroom.

He walks over to the table and grabs the money she left him. He counts it. It is $5.

He shakes his head as he plops down on the couch. He counts it again as he shakes his head in disappointment.

CHAPTER 9

The back door to the ground floor of the building is open. The hallway is narrow but well lit. There are two apartments on opposite sides of the hallway that leads to a slightly larger area with one apartment and a flight of stairs. The stairs lead to the upper two levels and a landing that is the front door. Light Skin, M.T., Derrick, Earl, Donny, Rob, O.G., Madness, Crud, and Lil Man are huddled in front of the steps, shooting dice. M.T. is stooped down and Light Skin is towering above him in the center.

The dice roll and five shows on one dice and three shows on the other dice. M.T. wins! In celebratory fashion, he scoops up $600 off the floor near his foot. There is $2000 piled up on the center of the floor. He starts laughing as he pumps his fist in the air before shaking hands with Rob and Earl. Earl and Rob collect money from the bets they just won from a few of the other men. Other winners and losers transfer money.

M.T. stops and looks at Light Skin braggadociously. *"You trying to win some of that five-grand back? Bet* *another $300?"* He says boisterously.

"Your point 6, right? Bet $500 on 6/8." Light Skin says in a tone that means Money doesn't mean a thing. Both men count off $500 and M.T. hands his to Light Skin.

"Bet. You work for me now!!!" M.T. shouts in pure excitement. He rolls the dice and when they stop, they both equal 6. He leaps up and grandstands in front of Light Skin, smiling. *"Ain't nothing like drug money, Baby."* He brags.

Light Skin frowns and shoves the money in M.T.'s hand. *"Shit! I just lost $6500 in here. Somebody else fade him. I'm betting with him."* He says with disappointment and amusement as he walks into the crowd.

Crud immediately steps up and tosses 5 $100 bills on the ground. He motions to stoop but stops. He pulls his gun from its uncomfortable position in the waist of his pants and sticks it in his pocket. *"You right! Ain't nothing like drug money as long as it's rent money. Shoot your heart out, M.T."* Crud barks boisterously.

M.T. just stares disappointingly at him. Crud stands and looks at him. *"What? What's wrong with you? My money ain't good?"* Crud says with confusion.

"Crud, why you got that with you? You youngsters be lunchin." He says as he waves his finger toward the gun.

"Laws of the street. I'd rather be caught with it, than without it. Everybody can't afford bodyguards like you and Light Skin," he says waning his hand in the direction of Madness, Rob and Earl, *"So I protect me with hollow points. Are*

you gambling or passing the dice?" He boasts.

Everybody except M.T. burst into laughter. M.T. smirks as he scans the room.

"That's right, Crud! You got him scared now! If he won't let you fade him, Crud, I will now." Light Skin laughs. "His heart gone. You took his heart, Crud!" Light Skin says as he grabs his stomach in intense laughter.

Crud steps closer to M.T. and stares into his eyes, jokingly. "Now I'ma take his money." He replies.

The others continue to laugh.

M.T. jokingly smirks. *"Yeah, o.k. I have no problem taking your little $500 you made today. You can always get a package from me!"* M.T. jokingly barks trying to win some laughter in his favor. He then stoops and shakes the dice in his hand. He stops and looks at Light Skin. *"Bet $200 I hit my point?"*

Light Skin nods his head in agreement.

"What? My money ain't good enough?" Crud says.

"Bet." M.T. says in a matter-of-fact tone as he counts off $200 and tosses it at Crud's feet. He rolls a 3. Light Skin, Crud, and a few of the other men YELL in Laughter as Crud snatches up all the money off of the floor.

CHAPTER 10

The sunlight streams through the thin blinds in Mrs. Janice's living room. Slim is asleep bald up in a sheet on top of a blanket on the floor. He is sandwiched in between the coffee table and the couch. No part of his body is visible.

Mrs. Janice walks out of her bedroom into the living room, singing and swaying her upper body. *"Nobody can love you more than Jesus. Je-s-us."* She sings heartfelt.

Slim rolls over and angrily snatch the sheet off of his head and bare chest. *"Ma!"* He shouts, glaring up at her.

Her eyebrows shoot upwards and her body responds with attitude. *"Whatever it is, it better begin with good morning, Beautiful."*

His facial expression softens. *"Good morning, Ma,"* he says with reluctance.

She frowns at him as she grips her waist.

"I mean, good morning, Beautiful." He says, smiling.

"Good morning, Handsome. Tell me, have your dreams

begun to help you find a job?" Mrs. Janice says, sarcastically.

"Huh?" He responds with confusion.

"My point exactly. It is 10am on this glorious Tuesday morning. It's time for you to begin your search. Do you have any leads?" She says with even more sarcasm and a smile.

"Yea, a construction company. Let me get up." He says as he sits.

CHAPTER 11

The noon sky is clear. The sun is out. There are a few dozen people walking around and purchasing heroin from a few different drug dealers standing in front of The Fair apartments but outside of the open entrance gate. Crud and Little Man are near each other selling their product. Crud is making three sells. O.G. is also making two sells. Angel is also serving a customer, but she is inside of the gate with her back to them. She is a very pretty brown skin sixteen-year-old with shoulder length black hair. She has on a man's style sweatsuit.

A new BMW pulls to the curb and park in front of them. Derrick and Donny exit the car. Derrick is carrying a brown paper bag. They start walking toward Crud. He spots them and head in their direction. Little Man looks over to them as if he is going to follow Crud until another addict approaches him. He scans the area then begins to take the junkies money in exchange for two bags of heroin.

Light Skins' Range Rover pulls to the curb and parks six cars up from the entrance of the buildings. He and Madness exit the car. Madness has on his trademark all black clothing and dark sunglasses. Light Skin calls Angel's name. She looks over and recognizes him. She starts walking toward the back of his truck.

Derrick, Donny, and Crud walk inside of the entrance gate and over to the first apartment building on the right; Mrs. Janice's building. There are only two apartment buildings on opposite sides of the front entrance. The walkway in between them leads to a

short flight of stairs that
reveals the countless
apartment buildings that
surround the playground,
basketball court and the
outdoor swimming pool.

Madness walks over
to O.G. They nod to each
other in greeting.

"What's up, Youngster?"
O.G. says.

*"Nothing much. I'm just
trying to see how your man
Slim feels."* Madness
replies with suspicion. His
hands are held together
behind his back. He scans
the area on both sides of
him.

"We're all family and that's where that starts and ends." O.G. says with conviction.

"You sure?" Madness says staring at him without any real emotions, but menace lies in his response and O.G. knows this.

"I said it, didn't I? Look, ya were cool. He treated you like his little brother before he went away. Shit changed. He understands that now. I will say that... you really went hard on him. He was more hurt than angry." O.G. says not backing down but not being aggressive.

"I'ma grown ass man. I don't care who you is, you don't rub my motherfucking head like I'ma five years old." Madness says in his calm menacing tone.

"Do you have any more of that Santa Claus?" Praise says as she interrupts Madness and O.G.'s conversation. She's a beautiful short woman with tan skin and a long ponytail, but she's slumped over. She looks sickly. Her hair is unkempt, but her clothes are clean.

Madness looks irritated by her interruption, but he looks

away. O.G looks down at the woman. *"Yea. How many you want?"* He says, calmly.

"Three." Praise replies with pleading eyes.

O.G. scans the flow of traffic before pulling out five half a dollar size zip-lock bags of heroin. He hands 3 of the small bags to Praise. *"Where my money at?"* He says.

She reaches into her pocket and hands him three bald up $20 bills.

"You used to be fine as shit. You still fine but you fading, Baby." He says flirtatiously as she sniffs

the bags and starts a little dance.

Crud pulls a stack of money out of his sleeve and hands it to Donny. Derrick is scanning the area. *"That's the whole six grand. Three from me and three from Little Man."* He says.

Derrick hands Crud the paper bag. Crud looks into the bag and sees $10000 worth of heroin in it.

"The same, right?" Crud says excitedly.

"Hit me up if you run out today." Derrick says before walking off. Donny walks off right beside him.

The sound of speeding cars coming from both directions can be heard.

"Jump outs!!!!!" O.G. screams from the top of his lungs.

Two unmarked police cars skid to a halt in front of them. Detective Anderson, Detective Flowers, Detective Jenkins, Detective Malls, and four other undercover cops leaps out of their cars and sprint toward different groups of junkies and hustlers. Angel along with a dozen others dashes in mostly opposite directions. Detective Malls chases her through the apartment gates.

Crud sprints in the same direction of Angel but behind Detective Mall before making a sharp right turn, while clutching the bag in his hand. Detective Jenkins races behind him. Light Skin slowly raises his hands in surrender as he steps away from his truck. Madness starts walking away from the area. Detective Flowers whips out her gun and runs up behind him. O.G. drops his remaining two bags of heroin on the ground and walks toward the gates at the entrance. The other officers wave their guns in the direction of the other people and demand them to get against the gate where O.G. is standing. Detective Anderson smiles as he walks over to Light Skin.

"I feel honored that you could join us today. Is this my lucky day, Mr. Light Skin?" Detective Anderson says sarcastically with a huge smile.

Light Skin smirks and places his hand behind his head. *"Only if you planting drugs today."*

Detective Anderson smiles as he signals Light Skin to turn around before he begins his search.

Angel is like ten paces away from Detective Mall, but he is gaining on her. She brushes pass a bush and eases a few bags of heroin out of her hand into it as she passes.

Detective Jenkins is nearing the playground area. Crud is fifty yards away from him. There is no way this guy is catching this kid. Crud is still clutching the brown paper bag full of dope. He scans back every so often to measure their distance.

Detective Flowers is still a few inches behind Madness with her gun aimed at the back of his head. He is standing still with his palms and fingers open a few inches away from his body

"I gave you a direct order, Madness!!!" She shouts.

"I'm not a damn cop. I don't know what that shit means." He says emotionlessly.

"Lock your hands behind the back of your head and get down on your knees now! This is your final warning!" She shouts.

"I'm not getting on no damn ground. I don't have shit." He says with irritation.

"Madness!! Get down on your knees." She bellows as she locks in her firing stance.

"Detective Flowers, I already told you, I aint doing that. I don't have any drugs. I don't have no weapons. I don't have nothing. You wasting yo time. Now you can search me but I...ain't getting on no fucking ground or moving so your trigger-happy ass can shoot me." He says.

Detective Jenkins is bent over by the outdoor pool, gasping for air. Crud is nowhere in sight.

Detective Mall apprehends Angel by the arm as she turns into a court. She tries to jerk away from his grip, but he holds onto her. He forces her against the wall.

"Stop resisting! You are not getting away and I am not going to hurt you. Just assume the position." He warns.

She stops. He searches her and finds nothing but a roll of money. He holds the money up in front of her.

"I didn't do anything… that's my mother's money." She pleads.

"Angel, I am not even going to go into this with you." He says.

"What? You didn't find anything on me." She shouts.

He waves the money in front of her. *"Tell me the exact dollar amount or it's mine."*

"It's $750. It's our rent money. My mother told me to hold it."

He leans his body against her, gently forcing her flat against the wall. He starts counting the money. It's $750 exactly. He steps away from her. She turns around and extends her hand out for the return of her money.

"Bye." He says.

"What? That's how much it is. I know that's how much it is." She says confidently but with a whine.

"Well, tell your mother to bring the paystub down to the precinct and I'll return the money." He says as he starts to walk off. She stares at him in disbelief.

Detective Flowers still has her gun aimed at the back of Madness' head. Detective High is finishing up his aggressive search of Madness. He locks eyes with Madness. "He's clean." He says.

Then Madness turns around and smiles at her before walking toward Light Skin and Detective Anderson.

Light Skin has his hands locked behind his head. Detective Anderson is searching his pockets. He retrieves a $10 bill from inside Light Skin's front pocket. He holds it for Light Skin's view. Light Skin smiles. *"And ya think I'm a kingpin."* He says sarcastically smiling.

CHAPTER 12

Construction equipment, construction workers and construction trucks are moving non-stop along this block long development site. The new structure of a six-story building is being built in the middle of a housing community. Light dust is in the air. Positioned on one end of the site is a long trailer. Slim exit the trailer. He is followed by the foreman, middle ages, chubby white guy with dirty brown hair. The man holds a clipboard in his hand. He talks at Slim as they head toward the exit. Slim is dressed in two sizes too big button-down shirt, tie, slacks and dress shoes. The foreman gestures to a man working on a light fixture on the second floor of the structure before stopping as he and Slim reaches the exit gate. He extends his hand to Slim.

"I want to thank you for coming. I will put your resume on file. I am not sure if we will need any more labors on this job. Now as soon as one of the 19 guys we just hire doesn't work out, we may give you a call. Now a lot of guys think they can do this work, but they sure find out that it's a lot harder than they thought. You're a

small guy. You think you can handle this backbreaking work? It's hard work?" The Foreman says humorously.

Slim smiles at him, *"I'm a lot tougher than I look."*

"I don't doubt that.," He says as he looks at Slim's resume. *"You seem like a really nice guy. You haven't had a job in a lot of years. Plus, the last job you worked was as a salesclerk. Was this a summer job?"* He questioned.

Slim looks down at the man's feet. *"Yes, Sir."*

"So, you received your G.E.D. two years ago? What have you been doing to take care of yourself since your summer job?"

Slim looks him back in his eyes, almost apologetically. "*In all honesty, Sir; I had chosen the wrong path for a while. Now I'm trying to get my life on the right track. I'm looking for a career, that's why I am here. I know I don't have any real work experience, but I am a good learner. I follow directions and I am dependable.*"

"*I don't mean any harm. I've heard that script before. I want you to think about what you just said to me. Well, can you repeat it to me."* The foreman replies.

Slim looks skeptical, *"I said that I am a good learner. I follow directions and I am dependable."*

"Now I'm not trying to be an asshole but like I said, I heard that before. In fact, several times. I don't mean to pry. I really want to help you understand my point. You've been to prison before, right?" The foreman says with sincerity.

Slim stares into his eyes before slowly

nodding his head. *"Yes."*
He replies.

"I figured that by your resume, and it was confirmed with what you just told me. I don't know why they teach ya'll that garbage. Look, young man, when you go on your next job interview, you explain to the manger how you can do the job and not that you're a fast learner. Those lines say nothing to me, but don't hire you. I don't mean to be a jerk. I just want you to get employed so you don't go back down that wrong path. Now I will keep your resume on file. Some of you guys who've been to prison are good workers and some of you

aren't worth crap. I'm looking at you and I think you may be one of the good ones." He smiles before extending his hand.

Slim shakes his hand.

"Good luck, Mr." The Foreman says as he pats Slim on the back. Then he walks off.

Slim stare at him with a look of confusion.

CHAPTER 13

The sun is starting to disappear from the sky and above the 24-hour community store. Madness is reclined in the passenger seat of Light Skin's truck. His shades are on and he is watching three men talking in front of the store. He nonchalantly holds an automatic handgun on his knee. He glances to his left and right at the two park cars on opposite sides of the truck.

Light Skin exit the store looking as if he is reading the newspaper in his hand. He has a white plastic bag with two bottles of water in it, dangling from his finger. He climbs into the truck and holds the newspaper toward Madness.

"Did we make the paper?" Madness says with dry humor and pride as he sits up and grabs the end of the paper that is directed toward him.

"You always make the paper. It's in the Metro Section. Before you read it, I want you to read that story in there about the city council trying to increase the school budget. Here." Light Skin says as he releases the newspaper and hands him one of the bottles waters.

Both men place their waters into the cup-holders. Madness starts flipping through the newspaper with childlike excitement. *"I don't want to read about that shit. I want to read about me."* He replies.

Light Skin smirks. *"I'm driving, so read that for me."* He says with a tone that Madness understood as him not playing around. Madness sighs. Then he starts reading the paper to him.

CHAPTER 14

The sky has become a mixture of purple and blue as the sun begins to settle. A man walks out of the corner store and around the side of the building. Crud is leaning against the front of a parked car. Little Man, Tye, and Berry are standing around him, rapping.

"So, you're in the wrong field/ trying to eat from a drug deal/I know your heart is soft/ so you bound to squeal/ That'll get u kilt" Tye barks through rapping.

"I love the streets/So I'll bang that heat/ Keep the neighborhood scared/So that's how I eat!" Little Man says boisterously as he raps.

"Ima killa, ain't goin fake it/If my hustle in the streets don't get it/I'ma take it/I'll blast on you faggots. Bang! Bang! I got'em /Call me Berry you Bastards. Whoop! Whoop!!" Berry says with gun gesturing before spinning toward Crud with victory in his voice.

Crud gives him a high five. They all start laughing. *"Damn. Damn. That was fiya!"* Crud says with a look that says he is impressed.

"Yea. We got to get back in the studio and finish that album." Tye replies with hope.

"We're gon to do that. I'ma try to book some studio time next week after I pay my share of the rent, then I'll know how many hours to book." Little Man says reassuringly.

"People need to hear the real and that's what ya' do." Crud says with bravado.

"We just showing them how we live." Little Man says in a calmer tone.

Donny and Derrick walk over to them. *"Little dirty and the slow learners. What's up, Shawty. Ya still studio Gangsters? Who ya kill on tracks this time?"* Donny says, jokingly. They laugh. Then Donny shakes all of their hands. Crud hand is the last one he shakes. He holds Crud's hand. Derrick shakes the rest of the teenagers' hand. *"Yo' little ass got away from them this morning!! I thought fo-Sho he was going to catch you!!!"* Donny says humorously.

"Sheed. He almost had me. I had to throw that damn bag you gave me! After he went for that, I kept

getting up." Crud says as he laughs.

Donny's smile vanishes. *"You did what?"* Donny barks in anger as he steps within inches of Crud's nose.

Crud smile vanishes as he stares back at Donny with no fear. *"I kept getting up."* He responds.

Derrick steps up to Crud. Now they have him blocked in. *"Why in the fuck would you throw the package?"* Derrick demands.

Crud stares seriously into his eyes. *"I wasn't getting caught with it. That was the only way I got away. Would you prefer that I got caught with it? I didn't.*" Crud says before his eyes drifting towards Derrick's throat.

Derrick leans his eyes closer to Crud's. "*I would of preferred if you didn't throw the dope. Shawty, that was ten grand worth of shit?*" He says through clenched teeth.

"*Looks like you gonna have to work that off.*" Donny says.

Crud looks him into his eyes. "*No, I don't. Ya was there. Ya saw them jump out. Ya saw him chase me."* Crud replies in almost a whining voice.

"Yea but I didn't see him come back with that bag." Derrick says with suspicion.

"You should of went to jail with that, that way you wouldn't have to work that off." Donny replies.

Crud frowns as he leans his upper body back away from them. *"I'm not going to jail to please you. And I'm not working for free. Ya was there so it ain't like ya didn't see it happen."* Crud says with conviction.

Donny pulls Derrick away from Crud. *"Oh, you are going to work that off."* Derrick says.

"Sheed. No, I am not." Crud replies.

CHAPTER 15

O.G. and Slim are in Rachel's car on a side street. O.G. is running his right hand repeatedly across the top of the steering wheel. Slim is seated reclined on the passenger seat, staring out of the window in a daze.

"You put in 6 job applications today!?" O.G. says in disbelief.

"Yup. Plus, I had two on the spot job interviews." Slim says with exhaustion and disappointment.

"How do you think they went?"

Slim sighs and shakes his head. *"I didn't get'em. Felony record."*

"The white man isn't going to let you become legit. We are still being oppressed. Before I ever had been arrested, I had a degree in communication. And I have NEVER had a job that wasn't entry level. That's when I woke up. We slaves, Youngster. We are still a part of the American dream. Slaves. First it was whips and chains. Now it's chains and cages."
"Yea." Slim says as he smirks with a hint of

sarcasm that says, here
we go again.

With an intense
look, O.G. stops and just
stares at him. *"I'm serious.
You better wake up. If you
ever want to ever get out
of your Mama's House,
you're going to have to
holla at Light Skin. Snatch
you a quick ten thousand
and go on your own."*

"I'm done with that shit."
Slim says with
determination.

*"So, what are you going to
do?"* With genuine interest
O.G. replies.

Slim adjusts himself
in the seat. *"I'm not selling*

drugs. Why is it taking you so long to get me a gun?" He ends with irritation.

"Despite what the newspapers may have you to believe, guns ain't as easy to come by. But I'm working on getting you something."

CHAPTER 16

Crud is leaning back on the couch playing video games. He is rocking back and forth with the controller in his hands and he frantically presses buttons. The window blinds are open and the moonless sky towers in the background. Near his feet on the floor is the console and video games. He glances over and down the long narrow hallway at the door as he hears the front door unlock and open. Little Man walks into the hallway with a bag of groceries. *"I need to holla at you."* He says in a serious tone.

"I'm not going nowhere...What's in the bag?" Crud says as he continues to play the game.

Little Man walks into the kitchen and starts putting the food away. "Cereal, milk, bacon, eggs, bread, and some chips."

"Let me get some chips...Did you take the rent to the rental office?

"That's done. They said, they're coming tomorrow morning to fix the heat." Little Man replies as he puts a gallon of milk into the refrigerator. Then he grabs the chips and walks into the living room and tosses the chips to Crud. Crud catches them. *"Thanks. Did they say what time they coming so one of us can be here?"*

"They said between 9:30 and 12: 00 so that means around 2:30." He says with humor.

"Well, that's not going to mess up the grind in the morning." Crud says half-jokingly.

Little Man stops beside him. *"Why are you running game, Crud?"* Little Man says with annoyance.

"What? What are you talking about?"

"I'm talking about you telling them that you threw the package." Little Man says.

"Fuck them. Why are you tripping off of them? Them dudes don't care nothing about you. They hand feeding us. You think they want us to get rich? Fuck naw." Crud replies dismissively as he continues to focus on playing the game.

"Crud, Man, we suppose to play-fair." Little Man says.

"Fuck playing fair! This is the drug game. Ain't no

*playing fair. Fuck them!
I'm going to take from
them every chance I get."*

*"Man, you're playing with
our rent money."* Little
Man responds.

*How you figure that? I just
took $10,000 worth of
heroin. Our rent money is
good."*

*"So, you don't think they're
not going to notice you
moving their shit?"* Little
Man replies.

*"Fuck them. Man, I'm going
to front it to Tye and them.
They don't work for Light
Skin; so, he won't know.
Plus, I'm only giving them
small packages at a time*

or sell them short shit. I got this. Chill out."

"But you still have to work that bill off for them so taking it doesn't make sense." Little Man says sarcastically.

"I don't work for free. Fuck them. They can act crazy if they want to, I'll knock more holes in their asses." Crud says as he whips an automatic handgun from the waist of his pants and holds it on his leg. Little Man looks at him and shakes his head with a look of bewilderment.

CHAPTER 17

Light Skin is reclined in the driver's seat of his Range Rover. Madness is relaxed and reclined in the front passenger seat. Derrick is standing outside of the truck talking to them, from Madness window.

"So how do you want to handle this?" Derrick asks leaning on the truck.

"We'll talk to him again." Light Skin replies.

"Cool. I like Shawty." Derrick says with his hands in his pockets.

"I like him too, but he can't be taking from us. But we will talk to him. Where is Donny?

"He wants to hit his head."

"Naw... I was asking, where is he?" Light Skin replies demandingly.

"He's on his way down here." Derrick replies.

      M.T. drives up beside the truck but behind Derrick and stops. He rolls down his window and smiles at Light Skin. Rob is visible on the passenger seat. The back window comes down and Earl smiles out at them.

"What'cha shooting for?" M.T. boasts.

"Whateva you want. Money talks." Light Skin replies, jokingly.

"Did you make any money today that you're willing to lose?" Derrick says, jokingly as Light Skin reaches down in the ashtray and grabs a pair of dice. He holds them up for M.T. to view.

"Let me park." M.T. says with urgency after looking at Derrick like he is a joke.

CHAPTER 18

Tye and Berry are standing outside of the apartment building, talking. Some other teenagers are walking pass them into the building. Crud and Little Man walk up to them and shake hands. *"What's up, Men."* Crud says.

"Love and happiness, Whoop! Whoop!." Berry says smiling. They all chuckle.

"Chilling. All of the big wigs are in the building gambling." Tye says as he nods his head in the direction of the building.

"Light Skin and the crew?" Little Man says with a look of caution.

"Yup. M.T. and his crew too." Tye responds.

Little Man looks over at Crud with a mixture of disappointment and discomfort.

"They had a $700 fade when I left up out of there. Whoop! Whoop!." Berry says.

"I'm going to get some of that money." Crud says with excitement.

"Did you bring that?" Tye says with a hopeful look.

"Yeah. Remember, I need ya' to keep people out of my business." Crud says with caution. Then he digs inside of the front of his pants, in his groin area and pulls out a brown sandwich bag. He hands the bag to Tye. *"I need two Gs back from both of ya".*

They nod their approval. Then a car horn beeps twice. Crud immediately snatches his gun from his front pocket and Berry snatches his gun from his waist. They both shield them next to their leg. Crud steps back into the shadow of the building. They are both prepared to fire them if need be. They all look to the car that pulled up.

"Whoop! Whoop!. Who is dat?" Berry says trying to peer into the car that is about 30 feet away from them.

"Little Man!!!" Aunt Charlene screams.

She beeps the horn again as she leans her head halfway out of the window. Then Little Man waves them off, *"That's my aunt."* He walks over to the car.

"Did one of them pull out a gun?" Aunt Charlene says with irritation.

"No, Aunt Charlene." He says as if he is shocked that she would ask such a bizarre question.

"I know what I saw. I told you about hanging with those thugs. And that was Crud too, that stepped back into the shadows? Who is he hiding from now?" She says with resentment.

"Ain't nobody hiding from nobody."

"Ain't? The correct pronunciation is, he is not hiding from anyone." She replies as she scans his eyes.

Little Man turns his upper body toward her. *"Aunt-"*

"Don't you talk back. Get in the car. I would like to talk to you." She demands.

He looks over to his boys as O.G. and Slim are walking up the block toward them. *"I'll be back."*

"Aight. Hi, Ms. Charlene!" Crud says as he leans forward so she can see his face.

She rolls her eyes. Little Man smirks and runs around the car. He gets in the front passenger seat. She drives off. *"Boy, I know you are not trying to ride in my car without your seatbelt on? Put that damn seatbelt on... now!"* She barks.

Crud looks at Slim as if he is sizing him up. *"I heard you was a gangster back in the day."*

O.G. starts lagging. *"He was only gone for three years!!"*

"So, you still a gangster or has prison made you soft." Crud says half-jokingly.

"Crud, right?" Slim says.

"That's right." Crud says proudly.

"Nice name." Slim says sarcastically as he extends

his hand. Crud shakes it and smiles.

Earl walks out of the building and heads toward M.T.'s car. *"Ya not getting in the game?"* Earl says as he continues to walk over to the car and opens the back door.

O.G. looks to Tye. *"What game?"* O.G. questions.

"They shooting in the building." Berry replies.

"I'm going to get some of that money." O.G. says as he briskly scales the steps and gestures with his head for Slim to follow

him. They walk into the
building.

CHAPTER 19

Aunt Charlene is still cruising through the neighborhood with Little Man in the front passenger seat. He has the seat reclined back to the point where his head is not viewable in the front passenger seat.

"When was the last time you have been to school?" She questions.

He turns uncomfortably in his seat. *"I've been."*

"I don't mean driving pass it. Baby, you need an education. Do you realize

how important it is? Can you read?" She says glancing seriously at him

He swings forward from his seat. *"What? Yea. What makes you think that I can't?"* He says with a look of disbelief and a tone of annoyance.

The car stops at a stop sign. She leans over and grabs a brochure out of the glove compartment. She hands it to him. *"Ok, read this."* She demands.

"Come on, Auntie." He says staring at her in total disbelief.

"If you can read, just read a paragraph for me." She says with a smile that is more of a smirk.

He shakes his head with a look of disappointment. Then he scans the brochure with his finger. *"CONTACT VISITS' mission is to assist at- risk youth, prisoners and ex-offenders to transition back into the community as productive members of society."* He smiles victoriously at her as he places it back into the glove compartment.

She reaches over and caresses his cheek. *"I do not want you to become one of those guys in this program. I love you, Little Man. I just need you to know that you can be either a great Blackman or you can become a shame to your family and friends. I am not here to preach to you but I really do love you."* She says with deep concern.

"I know. I love you too, Auntie. I'm going to be all right. I wanna comeback home and stay with you again. Things are getting rough. I just want to get away from all of this. I want to come home." He says sitting up and toying with his knee.

She whips the car over and parks at the curb. She wipes her crying eyes before snatching off her seatbelt and trying to hug him. Then she jerks his head toward her by his chin as she stares with a glowing smile. *"You. Yes. Yes. Yes. You can come home tonight.*

He lowers his eyes. *"Not tonight. I need to talk to Crud and let him know. I'll move back in tomorrow."*

"Baby, you do not owe him anything." She says without regret.

"I do. That's my best friend and we pay all the bills together. I'm just tired. I'll talk to him tonight and pack my stuff. Drop me off home." He says with a sense of sorrow.

She kisses him on his lips. Then she put her seatbelt back on. *"I am so proud of you."* She drives off.

CHAPTER 20

Slim, O.G., M.T., Donny, Derrick, Tye, Madness and Crud are all hovering over Light Skin and Berry in the hallway. Berry scoops up the money that is scattered around in front of some of the men's feet on the floor. Crud is happily taking the money from the hand of some of the other men. There is a pair of dice on the floor. One of the dice is showing one dot and the other is showing three. Light Skin looks disappointed because he just lost some money.

However, Berry has a handful of money.

"Make'um feel it where it hurts!" Crud barks.

"I got'um, Baby. Whoop! Whoop! You fading me, Light Skin?" Berry says pointing to the floor as he stares into Light Skin's eyes.

"Naw." Light Skins says in defeat as he stands.

"Scared money don't make money! Whoop! Whoop!" Berry says braggingly to the crowd.

"Shoot $300." M.T. says as he tosses the money on the floor. Berry counts off

$300 and tosses his money on the floor as well. *"Let me see them dice for a minute."* M.T. says with suspicion.

Berry hands him the dice as Crud counts his money towards the ceiling with a look of glee. *"Somebody that you know knows magic!"* He brags.

M.T. shakes the dice and rolls them across the floor. Crud swoops up the dice and stares threateningly at M.T. Then he hands them back to Berry. *"What kind of games you playin?"* Crud demands.

*"Don't trip. Whoop!
Whoop! Nothing can
change fate. Somebody
don't want to lose their re-
up money! Whoop! Whoop!
Coming out!"* Berry yaps
as he shakes the dice in
the air.

M.T. gestures for
him to stop. *"Bet another
two hundred you miss your
new point."* Berry throws
two hundred dollars down
next to the rest of the
money.

*"Anybody else don't believe
in my man?"* Crud happily
says holding money in the
air.

Madness holds up a
$50 bill. Donny and

Derrick holds up $20s.
Earl holds up a $20. Then
Light Skin holds up a
hundred-dollar bill. Crud
nods his approval to all of
them. Then he pats Berry
on his back. Berry shakes
and then rolls the dice.
The Dice equal eleven.
*"Whoop! Whoop! Ladies
and Gentlemen, we have a
motherfucking winner!
Whoop! Whoop!"* He says
dancing before him and
Crud start snatching up
their winnings.

M.T. throws his
hands in the air in defeat
as he walks into the
crowd. *"I'm done."*

"I been done." Light Skin says jokingly. Everybody else agrees with them.

Crud and Berry give each other high fives and throws themselves at each other like punk rockers.

"Whoop! Whoop!" Crud shouts jokingly.

Slim smiles proudly at him. O.G. pats them on the back at the same time. Everybody starts to make their way down the steps except for Light Skin and Madness. They linger back against the wall.

Berry looks suspiciously around at them. *"Whoop! Whoop!*

What's up?" Berry questions them with suspicion.

"We getting ready to holla at Crud." Madness says with attitude as he stares daringly into his eyes.

Berry looks at Crud to see if he wanted him to leave.

"I'm good. I'll rap to you tomorrow...what's up, fellas?" Crud says smiling.

Madness looks at Berry with a look that says, I am waiting for you to get the fuck on about your business.

Berry walks up the steps. He looks back a few times and sees Madness still staring at him.

Light Skin smiles and walks over to Crud. *"I heard you threw 6 grand that you owe to me."* Light Skin says calmly.

"Sure did. That's what it took to get Jenkins off my back." Crud says with a matter of fact tone.

"But you got away, Crud. Now you know I can't take that lost. So, you have any suggestions?" Light Skin says calmly without the smile.

"Naw. Unless you can write it off on your taxes." Crud replies, not looking at him but counting his winnings.

Madness steps and stands inches away from Crud's nose. *"I see you got jokes but no money. Either you going to come up with that 6 grand you owe or tomorrow you're going to work that off."*

"Madness, why you all in my face. I ain't scared of you." Crud replies with a look of nervousness.

Light Skin steps in between them. Madness steps back but keeps his eyes locked on Crud's eyes. *"Crud, I like you. So,*

I'm going to let you sleep on it. I know tomorrow you'll have a change of heart, if not, we-. Crud, just reconsider. You'll make a few hundred dollars off of the packages. I'm not going to let you starve. Just reconsider."

"There is nothing to reconsider. I threw the package. You were there. You saw them chase me. I don't understand why ya' coming at me like this. But I'm not putting my freedom on the line for a few hundred dollars." Crud says with defiance.

Light Skin nods his head in agreement. Crud shakes his head and he has a look of disbelief. He walks up the steps. *"I like him. I want you to help him reconsider but leave him alone.*

Madness nods his head in agreement.

CHAPTER 21

M.T., Earl, O.G., Slim, Berry, Tye, Donny, and Derrick are standing around talking in front of the building that they were playing dice in. Donny, Derrick, and Earl are talking to each other separately from the other men. M.T. turns away from the pack after he answers his cell phone.

"I grew up watching you get money out here. Whoop. Whoop." Berry sincerely says to Slim.

"Did you learn "Whoop! Whoop!" from me?" Slim

says, jokingly. They all
start chuckling.

*"Naw, that's original.
Whoop! Whoop! I'm not on
no gay shit but you
Gangster. I remember you
getting money. Then you
started putting in that
hammer work. So, welcome
back. Whoop! Whoop!"*

*"I'm trying to get a job,
Berry. I'm not back."*

M.T. walks back
over to them. He is no
longer on his phone. Crud
joins them.

*"Yeah, o.k. It's money out
here. You'll be back. I'm
just saying it would be*

*good to have you. Whoop!
Whoop!"* Berry says.

"Fellas, I have to run…"
M.T. says before turning
to Slim, *"If you change
your mind and want to get
back in the game, holla at
me. I could use some
soldiers."*

Slim shakes M.T.'s
extended hand. *"I'm good.
I could use a hammer
though."* Slim replies.

Light Skin and
Madness walks out of the
building. Light Skin is
talking on his cell phone.

*"I can't help you with that.
You don't need a gun if*

you're not in the streets."
M.T. says sarcastically.

Crud walks over
beside Slim, *"I may be able
to help you with that."*

*"Naw, don't do that. He
doesn't need one."* M.T.
interjects.

"What?" Slim says startled.

*"Goodnight Men. Aight,
Crud."* Light Skin says with
a warning look to Crud.

Then M.T. walks off.
His men follow him. Crud
smirks. Then turns his
back to Light Skin. Light
Skin smiles then he walks
off with his men close
behind.

"Why would you need one of those if you're chilling?" Berry questions with a look that says, *you ain't fooling me.*

"I only want to keep me safe." Slim says before walking off.

CHAPTER 22

Whisper is a homely looking fifty-year-old white man with a red and black striped flannel shirt on. He opens the door and nods his approval of the men's entry. Light Skin and Madness nod their heads to him as a greeting as they enter. However, Light Skin nods his head in a dancing motion. Madness has on a backpack. They stop in between the two beds in the hotel room. Whisper locks the door. Then he gestures to them to have a seat on the bed nearest the door. They sit.

There is a midsize traveling bag with wheels laid across the bed close to them. Whisper goes and lightly knocks on the bathroom door. The door opens. The sound of sink water can be heard running lightly.

"They're here?" Rico says from the bathroom. He is a stylish short Columbian man with a slim built. Whisper nods in agreement. Then Rico steps out of the bathroom wearing only slacks. He is patting a washcloth on his face as if he just finished shaving. He steps into the area where the others are. The two men stand. He randomly pats his chin

with the washcloth. He walks over and shakes Light Skin's hand as he stands. *"I am delighted to see you again. How is your health?"* He says with a strong accent.

"I am well." Light Skin says as he smiles and nods his head with a look of respect.

Then Rico goes and embraces Madness with more affection as he kisses him on the cheek. He steps back and holds Madness by his shoulders. *"You have made my life so much better."* He gestures toward the room. *"Money, family, life and respect keeps...me...Happy. You have given me much happiness. Although it takes away some of my money, but it is money well spent. Thank you, My friend."* He says patting him on his shoulder before shaking hands again.

"You are welcome." Madness says with a forced smile.

Rico smiles at Whisper as he gestures back to Madness. *"He is so humble. This is why you are so good."* He says to Madness. Then he shakes Light Skin's hand again. *"You are ultimately responsible for my new respect for our relationship. You make me happy, My friend. Now let me uphold my end."* Rico goes and unzips the travel bag and pulls out an express size envelope and a shoebox. He sits the shoebox on the bed and hands the envelope to Light Skin. He shakes Light Skin hand again. *"Thank you again. Dis' man lacked respect for my money, his family, and his life. Why should he live? He had Whisper so upset. This is why I reached out to my friends to help us... With that being said, you made the newspaper."* He laughs as he walks over to the dresser and picks up the folded newspaper. *"This is the nicest thing his family*

*has probably heard said
about this garbage. He was
a family man. He should
have paid me my money!
And he would still be living
and taking care of his
family!!"*

Whisper walks over
and gently touches him on
his shoulder. *"Don't upset
yourself.* Then Whisper
grabs a bottle of water out
of the sink. He hands it to
him.

"Thank you, My friend..."
He takes a sip of the
water. *"Why the woman? I
thought she was your lady
friend. Don't answer this. I
already know. She knew
too much. Such is the
business we are in. You are*

not going to count your money?

If I didn't trust you, we wouldn't have killed for you." Light Skin says, half-jokingly.

Rico frowns as he gestures toward the ceiling. *"You never know who is listening...Also, my friend, situations change. Today I may not have been living so comfortably. He hurt my livelihood. It is so much of that going on these days that it is hard to stay in power unless you rob people of the American dream. At least look in there to see if it is money there."*

Light Skin opens the bag and pulls out a stack of money as he peers into the envelope. Then he puts the money back into the bag. *"I'll count it later. I just want to take care of the rest of our business."*

Rico smiles before opening the shoebox and placing two kilos of heroin on the bed. *"You Americans are always so in a rush. Never stopping to enjoy family and friends. This often disappoints me. This is why your families are dysfunctional.*

Light Skin walks over and picks up a kilo. *"I*

thought you hated Americans?"

"It is your government that I dislike. Because of Pablo they make Columbian's suffer...I love you, my friend, and I love all of my American customers. I am the American Dream. You could be too if you stop looking rich. Rico says jokingly as he waves at Light Skin's clothing.

CHAPTER 23

Slim and O.G. walk into Mrs. Janice's house. She comes walking out of the kitchen smiling but that quickly fades once she sees O.G. The two men are still standing near the door with conflicting looks.

"Hi, Mrs. Janice? You are looking as lovely as ever." O.G. says with humor as he walks toward her with his arms stretched out in an attempt to hug her. She gently pushes his hands away from her.

"You still can't find anyone your own age to play with I see." She replies.

Slim walks pass them and into the kitchen. *"Ma', he just wanted to use the bathroom."* Slim says with a hint of annoyance.

"So just let me guess, he just happened to be in the neighborhood and saw you walk up... just in time for him to use the bathroom. I am not buying it so please don't try to sell it to me. So, I guess you didn't go job hunting today?"

"As a matter of fact, he did, that's where I saw him. Could you believe we ended up at the same job opening?" O.G. says as Slim tries to signal him to be quiet.

"So, I guess now you have to put in a job application to sell drugs?" She says dismissively.

Slim walks to the edge of the kitchen near the two of them. *"Ma', I'm not selling drugs."*

She looks over at him, *"Then you must be considering it. Hanging out with him. I'm not having this out of you this time."*

"Can I use the bathroom?" O.G. says with irritation.

"Yes, as long as you don't hide none of that stuff in my bathroom." She warns.

"*Mrs. Janice, I am offended. I would never do such a thing.*" O.G. says in his most polite tone.

"*Boy! I mean, Old Man; you better go ahead into that bathroom. Then you have to leave, it is too late to be hanging out in somebody's home.*"

O.G. walks into the bathroom.

CHAPTER 24

Crud, Berry, and Tye are walking down the street along the neighborhood apartment buildings.

"Youngen, you know they're trying to knock these buildings down and build houses." Crud says with a look of disappointment.

"Whoop! Whoop! I know, that's why I'm trying to get my money right." Berry replies.

"My mother said they're not going to be able to do it. The tenants have to vote

and ain't nobody voting."
Tye says.

Berry starts
laughing. *"Youngin,
Whoop! Whoop! Everybody
around here on Section 8.
We don't have no say. The
white people trying to take
back over the city. They
getting our asses out!
Whoop! Whoop!"* Berry
says with confidence.

*"That's some true shit. Me
and Little Man going to
holla at my Mother to see if
she can get us another
spot."* Crud chimes in.

*"See if ya' can get her to
get ya' a three bedroom.
I'm trying to get out of my
Grandma's house! It's too*

many people up in there. Whoop! Whoop!" Berry says firmly.

"Berry, your ass ain't going to leave your grandmother. Stop faking." Crud says, laughing.

"Sheed. I'm going to make sure she aight and keep money in her pocket; but I have to get up out of there! Motherfuckers in my clothes, my shoes, my weed, you name it. Whoop! Whoop! Or see if somebody can help me get a spot. Whoop! Whoop!" Berry says seriously.

"Damn." Tye mumbles.

"I wish we can buy a building so nobody can put us out. We own our own shit and we put motherfuckers out! Whoop! Whoo!." He says excitedly.

They laugh.

CHAPTER 25

Mrs. Janice is shutting the refrigerator. O.G. is standing in the open doorway. He embraces Slim before disappearing into the hallway. Slim shuts the door and locks it. Then Mrs. Janice walks out of the kitchen as he pulls his cover, sheet, and pillow out of the closet. She is standing in the living room with her hands on her hips, watching him spread the sheet across the carpet right up against the couch.

"I thought you were going to do right this time. You just can't put any faith in

God." She says with disappointment and sorrow.

"Ma', ain't doing nothing."

"What you forgot, I went through this same stuff with your father. Why do you think we're not together? The two of you refuse to do right. Why you can't live right, Baby?" She says pleadingly.

He lays the pillow against the bottom of the couch. Then he turns to her. *"Ma', I ain't doing nothing. I'm looking for a job."*

"Then why are you with him! He doesn't want

*anything. You think he
cares about you! You must
be his flunky!"*

*"Ma', I ain't nobodies
flunky!"*

*"Well...if you're not his
flunky, you must be the
system's flunky! You're
never going to get away
with breaking the law!
You're* going to end up
spending the rest of your
life in jail or you're going
to get killed in these
streets!" She says with a
look of regret.

*"Ma', I'm not doing
nothing."* He says
reassuringly.

"Well, ok. This should work out fine. For now on, I want you in here by ten o'clock every night." She says firmly.

"What? Ma', I'm 26 years old. How you going to give me a curfew."

"This is not up for discussion. As long as you live in my house, you will abide by my rules. I want you in here by ten o'clock every night or don't come home. And if you spend the night out without letting me know in advance, I want you out of here! Do you hear me!" She barks.

He just stares at her in disbelief.

"Did you hear me?"

"Yes. I did." He says in almost a mumble.

CHAPTER 26

Crud spits over the curb as he walks down the street toward his building. He can see his building through the black gate that extends the length of the block. However, he is at least one building away from his building.

Little Man comes walking out of the building carrying a large trash bag.

"Hey!!!" Crud yells.

Little Man stops at the top of the steps and looks up and sees Crud walking closer to the entrance of the gate. He is still approximately 30 feet away.

"Where you going this time of night!" Crud says, half-jokingly.

"To empty the trash. You coming in the house!?" Little Man asks.

"Yeah."

Little Man nods his approval. Then he makes his way around the far side of the building where the community trashcans are located. He lifts the flap on the trash bins and tosses his bag inside. Madness steps out from the shadows behind him.

He walks up with his gun aimed at the back of Little Man's head...

Crud is three feet away from the entrance of the gate to his complex. One gunshot is fired. Crud instantly crouches down. He is looking wildly around. Another gunshot is fired. Crud swiftly moves over in between two parked cars to shield himself. Then he snatches the gun from his waist. He peeps out and spots Madness briskly walking out of the other entrance gate about 50 feet from his building with a gun in his hand. Then he hears a car door shut and the car drives off at a normal speed.

"Little Man!!!!!" Crud screams in despair as he sprints through the entrance gates to his building with a look of horror. He runs around to where Little Man walked.

THE END...TO BE CONTINUED

QUICK QUESTION

1. What are your thoughts on how they live their lives?

   _____
   _____
   _____
   _____

2. Which character's story interest you most and why?

   _____
   _____
   _____
   _____

3. What are your thoughts about Madness?_____

   _____

_____
_____
_____

4. **Who was your favorite character and Why?**

_____
_____
_____
_____

5. **Why do you believe they make the choices they make?**_____

_____
_____
_____
_____
_____
—

6. **What situation in the book you would have**

**handled
differently?**

_____

_____

_____

_____

7. **What is Mrs.
   Janice's issue with
   O.G.?**_____

_____

_____

_____

ADDICTED TO LOVE is the
next book in the Laws Of
The STREETS series.

Check out Lamont Carey's Predator or Prey prison series: There are three books in this series:

THE HILL

Follow Sherman as he begins serving his prison sentence at Lorton Correctional Compound. This complex house some of the deadliest men in the world. It's a penitentiary so dangerous that other maximum- security prisoners don't wanna go. Sherman made some bad choices in his life. Now he will either live or die from the consequences.

THE WALL is the sequel to the book THE HILL. It takes you to a prison more deadly and sinister than THE HILL. Real Gangsters have been known to scream behind...THE WALL. No one is safe. There are no leaders. Everyone is a killer.

First THE HILL - Then THE WALL - and now...
THE TRANSITION
FROM ONE HELLHOLE TO ANOTHER

FREEDOM ISN'T
EASY WITH
FELONY
CONVICTIONS

LAMONT CAREY

THE TRANSITION is the journey after Washington, DC's extremely violent prison system Lorton closes down. Some of the prisoners are released to the community and the rest, mostly young black males, are shipped to the federal prison system. They are in for a rude awakening. Freedom isn't easy with felony convictions. And the federal system isn't

Lorton. Their new home is run by the Aryan Brotherhood who would love nothing more than to slit their throats.

Other works by Lamont Carey:

  Dead Before 18 - Saving our boys from the Streets" is a navigational guide written to and for young boys who have and will face a complex world that demands making decisions and promises consequences. It is written from the perspective and experiences of the writer who made many mistakes while learning how to be a man.

The goal of the book is to make these boys and young men aware of the pitfalls, so they might avoid lives of self-destruction.

Reach Into My Darkness is a collection of narrative poems that mirror the readers' very own life's experiences and barriers. The goal of the book is to inspire self- reflection, self-expression and empowerment.

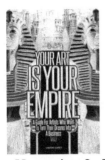

Your Art Is Your Empire is a guide for performing, recording, and spoken-word artists who want to turn their dreams into a business...and ultimately...an empire. The book covers such topics as: legal business structures, taxes, marketing, creating a bio, and creating their first product and more.

The Journal was created simply to assist you in reaching your personal and career goals. It comes complete with areas for goal setting and tasks to carry out. There are additional sections where you can journal and even draw pictures. It is great for programs and personal use.

Lamont Carey's award-winning CD containing such hits as "I Can't Read", "Confidence", "I Hate This Place", "She Says She Loves Me", and ten other electrifying spoken word pieces. Digital files are available for sale on iTunes, CD Baby, amazon and more.

T-Shirts

Keep Your Hustle but Change Your Product. The difference between illegal and legal is the product. Join the movement! Order your T-shirt from the website and help spread the word!

Creative Mind
 A Creative Mind Is A
Goldmine. Lamont
believes artist have the
ability to change the
world and make a living
off of their creations. No
more starving artist!
Order your T-shirt from
the website!
www.lacareyenterprises.c
om/clothing

Lamont Carey is an
international award-

winning spoken word artist, filmmaker, playwright, actor and motivational speaker. To make booking arrangements for speaking or performance engagements for your group, students, prisoners, employees, conferences, or at any other event you are having worldwide, contact LaCarey Enterprises, LLC: lacareyentertainment@yahoo.com

You may visit the website at: www.lacareyentertainment.com

Send fan mail to:

LaCarey Entertainment,
LLC P.O. Box 64256
Washington, DC 20029

CPSIA information can be obtained
at www.ICGtesting.com
Printed in the USA
LVHW090339040921
696898LV00002BA/63